FARMER TURNIP
BY BRIAN HOWES

PICTURES BY ROWAN BARNES-MURPHY

Old Farmer Turnip has very thin hair
And he feels very cold when his head is all bare,

So, going out Sunday, he searched all around
For his hat – but it couldn't be found.

He checked through the kitchen, the dining room too,

The front room,

the wash house

– and even the loo.

He asked his wife, Grace, who was sweeping the mat,
But she didn't know what he'd done with his hat.

He heard a strange noise on his way up the stairs.
In a cupboard he felt something covered with hairs.

But what he'd discovered was Bimbo, the cat,
Who scratched him and bit him – but not his old hat.

He looked through the bedrooms, the bathroom, the loft,
Where he found a brass parrot cage, a football gone soft,
A box full of costumes, and all sorts of tat,
But nowhere up there could he find his old hat.

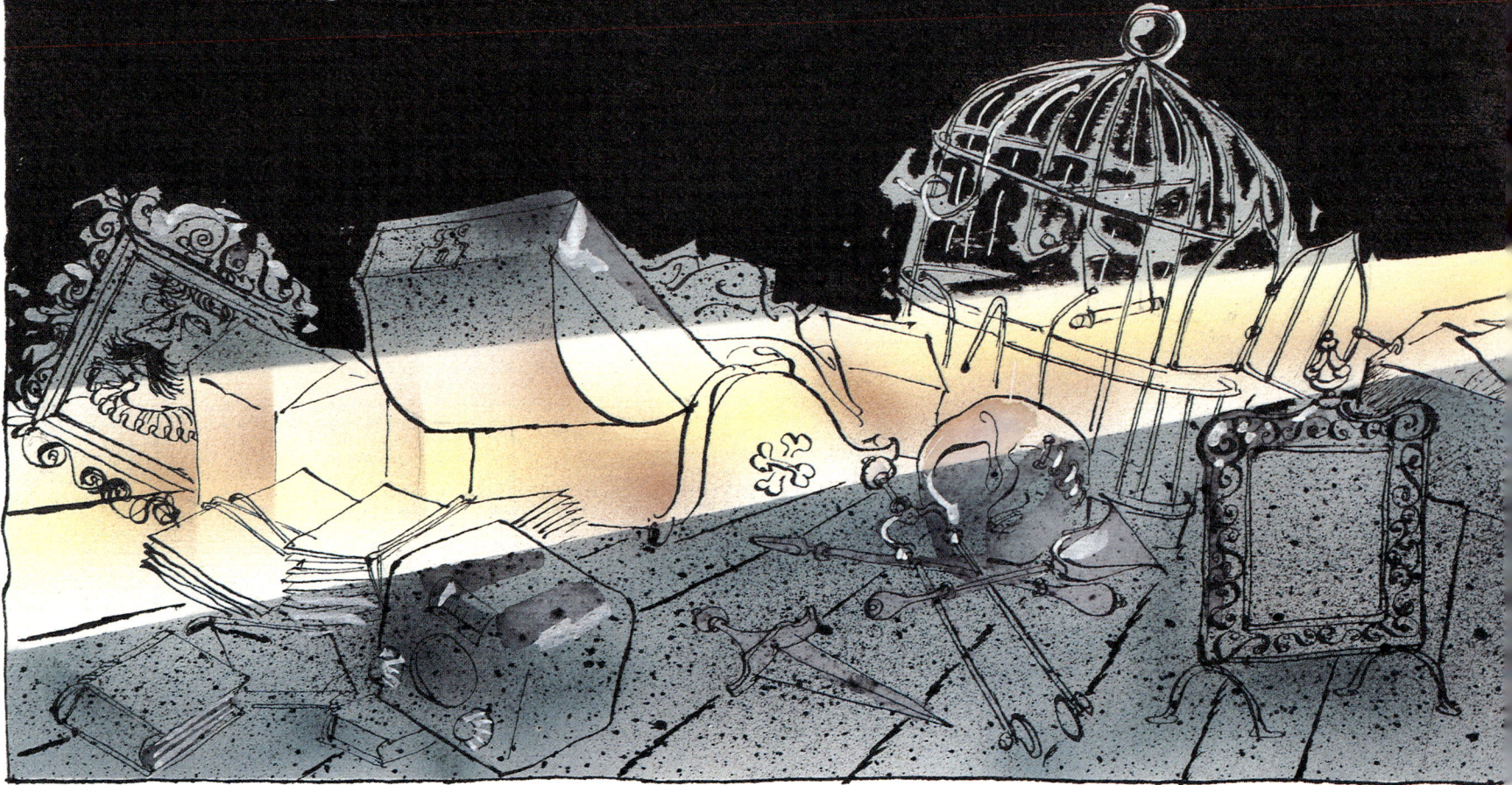

9

Back down the stairs he went, thinking quite hard,
Then out through the door, and across the farmyard.
What's that old Bonzo is chewing? He peered.
A slipper! – And not his old hat, as he'd feared.

He sat on the branch of a tree for a rest,
And he noticed a starling had built a strange nest.
The edge was all curly, the bottom quite flat.
He'd found his old hat! He'd found his old hat!
At last he had found it! He'd found his old hat!

Through leaves and branches he reached out his hand,
But the bird squawked as loudly as any brass band.
"All right," said the farmer, "I'll not take it down.
I shall buy a new hat when I go into town.
When I go into town, when I go into town."

"I shall buy a new hat when I go into town."

So he did!